NINJA FOODI MAX
SMARTLID
COOKBOOK
UK 2022
500

By:
Charlie Grace

TABLE OF CONTENT

Breakfasts

Fish & Seafood Recipes

Poultry Recipes

Lunch Recipes

Meat Recipes

Side Dish Recipes

Vegetable Recipes

Snack & Appetizer Recipes

Desserts

BREAKFAST RECIPES

1

CHICKEN CASSEROLE

Ingredients

- 450g chicken meat; ground

- 10 eggs

- 1 sweet potato; cubed

- 1 yellow onion; chopped.

- 15ml canola oil

- 3g garlic powder

- Salt and black pepper for the

  taste

Preperation

1. Set the Ninja Foodi Smartlid on Sauté mode, add the oil, heat it down, add the onion, stir and cook for just two-3 minutes. Add the meat, stir and brown for 3 minutes more.

2. Add all of those other ingredients, toss, set on Baking mode and cook at 175°C for 20 mins. Divide between plates and serve.

(PREP + COOKING TIME: 30 MINUTES | SERVES: 6)

2

CHEDDAR BEEF

Ingredients

- 450g beef meat; ground

- 1 red onion; chopped.

- 4 eggs; whisked

- 120g cheddar; grated

- 2g thyme; chopped.

- 15ml essential olive oil

- Salt and black pepper towards the taste

Preperation

1. Set the Foodi on Sauté mode, add the oil, heat it down, add the meat, stir and brown for 5 minutes.

2. Add onion, stir and sauté for 5 minutes more. Add the remainder of the ingredients except the cheese and toss.

3. Sprinkle the cheese towards the end, set the machine on Bake mode, and cook at 175°C for quarter-hour more. Divide between plates and serve in the morning.

(PREP + COOKING TIME: A HALF-HOUR | SERVES: 4)

3

BEEF HAM AND BUTTER SANDWICH

Ingredients

- 4 bread slices
- 4 cheddar cheese slices
- 4 beef ham slices
- 20g butter

Preperation

1. Spread the butter on each bread slice, divide the cheese along with the beef ham on 2 of these, top with all the other 2 and cut each in halves.

2. Put the sandwiches inside Foodi and cook on Air Fry for 8 minutes.

3. Divide the sandwiches between plates and serve enjoying.

(PREP + COOKING TIME: 13 MINUTES | SERVES: 2)

4

BELL PEPPER OMELET

Ingredients

- 4 eggs

- 75g bell pepper; chopped.

- 60ml coconut milk

- 120g cheddar cheese; shredded

- 1 red onion; chopped.

- 7ml organic olive oil

- A pinch of salt and black

  pepper

Preperation

1. Set the Foodi Max on Sauté mode, add the oil, heat it down, add the onion, stir and sauté for 5 minutes.

2. Add the remainder of the ingredients, toss, squeeze pressure lid on and cook on High for ten mins. Release pressure to ensure success fast for 5 minutes, divide the amalgamation between plates and serve.

(PREP + COOKING TIME: TWENTY OR SO MINUTES | SERVES: 4)

5

COCONUT SCRAMBLE

Ingredients

- 1 red onion; chopped.

- 4 eggs

- 60g cheddar; grated

- 60g coconut cream

- 15ml canola oil

- 15g chives; chopped.

- Salt and black pepper about the taste

Preperation

1. Set the Foodi on Sauté mode, add the oil, heat it down, add the onion, stir and sauté for two main-3 minutes. In a bowl, mix all of those other ingredients and whisk well.

2. Pour this about the onion, toss, set the unit on Air Fry and cook the scramble for ten mins, stirring the amalgamation halfway. Divide the scrambled eggs between plates and serve.

(PREP + COOKING TIME: 25 MINUTES | SERVES: 4)

6

FISH AND SEAFOOD RECIPES

7

SALMON AND BALSAMIC SHALLOTS

Ingredients

- 2 salmon fillets; boneless

- 80ml balsamic vinegar

- 4 shallots; chopped.

- 30ml organic essential olive oil

- 30ml lime juice

- Salt and black pepper around the taste

Preperation

1. Set the Foodi on Sauté mode, add the oil, heat it down, add the shallots and sauté them for 4 minutes. Add the lime juice, vinegar, salt and pepper, toss and cook for just two minutes more.

2. Add the salmon, place pressure to succeed lid on and cook everything on High for ten mins. Release pressure to ensure success fast for 5 minutes, divide between plates and serve.

(PREP + COOKING TIME: 17 MINUTES | SERVES: 2)

8

CREAMY SALMON BITES

Ingredients

- 450g salmon; boneless, skinless, and cubed
- 60g heavy cream
- 2 garlic cloves; minced
- 30g butter; melted
- 5g chives; chopped.
- Salt and black pepper for the taste

Preperation

1. Set the Foodi on Sauté mode, add the butter, heat, add the garlic and chives and sauté for just two minutes.

2. Add the remainder of the ingredients, squeeze pressure lid on and cook on High for 12 minutes. Release pressure to have success naturally for 10 minutes, divide between plates and serve.

(PREP + COOKING TIME: 25 MINUTES | SERVES: 4)

9

Ingredients

- 4 salmon fillets; boneless

- 90g butter; melted

- 10ml lime juice

- Salt and black pepper for the taste

BUTTER SALMON

Preperation

1. **Put the reversible rack inside the Foodi, add the baking pan inside and place the fish as well as other ingredients inside pan.**

2. **Set the product on Baking mode, cook at 187°C for twenty minutes. Divide between plates and serve with a side salad.**

(PREP + COOKING TIME: 25 MINUTES | SERVES: 4)

10

CREAMY SEA BASS

Ingredients

- 450g sea bass fillets; skinless, boneless, and cubed
- 250g coconut cream
- 1 red onion; chopped.
- 4g parsley; chopped.
- 5ml extra virgin essential olive oil
- Salt and black pepper towards taste

Preperation

1. Set the Foodi on Sauté mode, add the oil, heat up, add the onion and sauté for 4 minutes.

2. Add all the ingredients except the parsley, position pressure to succeed lid on and cook on High for 10 mins. Release pressure fast for 5 minutes, divide the fish mix into bowls, sprinkle the parsley ahead and serve.

(PREP + COOKING TIME: A QUARTER-HOUR | SERVES: 4)

11

HONEY SALMON CUBES

Ingredients

- 450gsalmon fillets; boneless, skinless, and cubed
- 60ml lime juice
- 15ml essential olive oil
- 30g honey
- Salt and black pepper around the taste

Preperation

1. Set the Foodi on Sauté mode, add the oil, warm up, add the salmon and also the most the ingredients, place the stress lid on and cook on High for ten mins. Release the stress naturally for 10 minutes, divide the into bowls and serve.

(PREP + COOKING TIME: TWENTY OR SO MINUTES | SERVES: 4)

12

POULTRY RECIPES

13

CHICKEN BOWLS WITH GREEN ONIONS SAUCE

Ingredients

- 450g chicken breasts; skinless, boneless, and cubed
- 250ml coconut milk
- 10 green onions; chopped.
- 4 garlic cloves; minced
- 45ml soy sauce
- 15ml fresh lemon juice
- 5ml extra virgin olive oil
- Salt and black pepper for the taste

Preperation

1- Set the Foodi on Sauté mode, add the oil, heat up and mix each of the ingredients except the chicken. Stir, cook the sauce for 5-6 minutes and then add the chicken.

2- Toss, squeeze pressure lid on and cook on High for quarterhour.

3- Release pressure to ensure success naturally for 10 mins, divide everything into bowls and serve.

(PREP + COOKING TIME: 30 MINUTES | SERVES: 4)

14

DUCK AND JELLY

Ingredients

- 450 to 900g duck, cut into pieces
- 1 yellow onion, sliced
- 120g red currant jelly
- 4 garlic cloves, chopped.
- 30ml extra virgin olive oil
- Salt and black pepper around the taste

Preperation

1- Put the reversible rack in the Ninja Foodi Smartlid, add the baking pan inside and mix all of the ingredients. Cook on Baking mode at 195°C for half an hour, divide between plates, and serve with a side salad.

(PREP + COOKING TIME: 40 MINUTES | SERVES: 4)

15

CHICKEN AND EGGPLANT STEW

Ingredients

- 450g chicken breasts, skinless, boneless, and cubed
- 1 big eggplant, cubed
- 120g tomato sauce
- 1 yellow onion, chopped.
- 2 garlic cloves, minced
- 30ml olive oil
- 4g parsley, chopped.
- Salt and black pepper about the taste

Preperation

1- Set the Machine on Sauté mode, add the oil, heat it down, add the onion and garlic and sauté for 5 minutes.

2- Add other ingredients, put the pressure lid on and cook on High for 25 minutes. Release pressure fast for 5 minutes, divide the stew into bowls and serve.

(PREP + COOKING TIME: 30 MINS | SERVES: 4)

16

HERBED CHICKEN AND TOMATOES

Ingredients

- 2 chicken breasts; skinless, boneless, and cubed
- 200g canned tomatoes; drained and chopped.
- 15ml freshly squeezed lemon juice
- 30ml extra virgin olive oil
- 5g garlic powder
- 3g thyme; dried
- 3g rosemary; dried
- 2g basil; dried
- Salt and black pepper for the taste

Preperation

1- Set the Foodi on Sauté mode, add the oil, warm up, add the chicken cubes and brown for 5 minutes.

2- Add all of those other ingredients, squeeze pressure lid on and cook on High for 20 mins. Release pressure naturally for ten minutes, divide a compounding into bowls and serve.

(PREP + COOKING TIME: 35 MINUTES | SERVES: 4)

17

WHITE CHICKEN STEW

Ingredients

- 450g chicken breasts, skinless, boneless, and cubed
- 280g cream of mushroom soup
- 1 yellow onion, chopped.
- 3g oregano, dried
- 5ml organic olive oil
- Salt and black pepper for the taste

Preperation

1- Set your Foodi on Sauté mode, add the oil, heat it, add chicken cubes along with the onion, stir and cook for 5 minutes.

2- Add the rest of the components, squeeze pressure lid on and cook on High for 20 minutes. Release pressure to achieve success naturally for 10 minutes, divide between plates and serve.

(PREP + COOKING TIME: 35 MINUTES | SERVES: 4)

18

LUNCH RECIPES

19

PESTO POTATOES

Ingredients

- 450g gold potatoes; cut into chunks
- 220g spinach pesto
- 60g parmesan; grated
- 3 garlic cloves; minced
- 1 yellow onion; chopped.
- 15ml organic olive oil

Preperation

1. Set the Foodi on Sauté mode, add the oil, heat up, add the onion, stir and sauté for 5 minutes. Add the garlic and also the potatoes, toss and cook for 2-3 minutes more.

2. Add the residual ingredients, toss, position the stress lid on and cook on High for quarter-hour. Release pressure to succeed naturally for ten minutes, divide the amalgamation into bowls and serve for lunch.

(PREP + COOKING TIME: 30 MINUTES | SERVES: 4)

20

SWEET POTATO STEW

Ingredients

- 450g sweet potatoes; cubed

- 340g tomato puree

- 3g marjoram; dried

- 30ml extra virgin olive oil

- Salt and black pepper towards

  the taste

Preperation

1. In your Foodi, combine each one of the ingredients, toss, squeeze pressure lid on and cook on High for 20 or so minutes. Release the stress naturally for ten mins, divide the stew into bowls and serve.

(PREP + COOKING TIME: HALF AN HOUR | SERVES: 4)

21

TOMATOES AND POTATO BAKE

Ingredients

- 420g gold potatoes; peeled and cubed
- 280g tomato sauce
- 60g cheddar cheese; grated
- 1g cilantro; chopped.
- 5g butter; melted

Preperation

1. Put the reversible rack inside Foodi, add the baking pan inside and add all the ingredients except the cheese inside the pan. Sprinkle the cheese at the very top, set your machine on Baking mode, cook the stew at 190°C for 25 minutes, divide it into bowls and serve.

(PREP + COOKING TIME: HALF AN HOUR | SERVES: 4)

22

SALMON AND FENNEL

Ingredients

- 2 salmon fillets; boneless
- 2 fennel bulbs; sliced
- 60g butter; soft
- 1g dill; chopped.
- Salt and black pepper for the taste

Preperation

1. Divide the butter on 2 parchment paper pieces. Divide the salmon along with other ingredients, toss and fold the packets.

2. Put the basket in your smarlid machine, add the packets inside and cook on Air Fry for 7 minutes on either side.

3. Unfold the packets, divide a compounding between plates and serve for lunch.

(PREP + COOKING TIME: 24 MINUTES | SERVES: 2)

23

BEEF MEATBALLS

Ingredients

- 450g beef; ground

- 190g tomato sauce

- 1 egg; whisked

- 1 yellow onion; chopped.

- 3g oregano; chopped.

- 15g basil; chopped.

- 15ml organic olive oil

- 15g breadcrumbs

- Salt and black pepper for that

  taste

Preperation

1. In a bowl, mix each one of the ingredients, except the tomato sauce combined with the oil, stir and shape medium meatballs using this mix.

2. Set the Foodi on Sauté mode, add the oil, get hot, add the meatballs and brown them for 5 minutes. Add the tomato sauce, toss, place the pressure lid on and cook on High for twenty or so minutes.

3. Release pressure naturally for 10 mins, divide between plates and serve.

(PREP + COOKING TIME: 35 MINUTES | SERVES: 4)

24

MEAT RECIPES

25

LAMB CHOPS AND APPLE SAUCE

Ingredients

- 4 lamb chops
- 2 garlic cloves, minced
- 120ml apple sauce
- 60ml extra virgin olive oil

Preperation

1- Put the reversible rack inside Foodi, add the baking pan inside and mix all the ingredients within the pan. Cook on Baking mode at 195°C for twenty minutes, divide between plates, and serve.

(PREP + COOKING TIME: 25 MINUTES | SERVES: 4)

26

BAKED THYME GOAT STEW

Ingredients

- 450g goat stew meat, cubed

- 250ml beef stock

- 2 garlic cloves, minced

- 2g thyme, chopped.

- 30ml extra virgin essential olive oil

- Salt and black pepper towards taste

Preperation

1- Put the reversible rack inside Foodi, add the baking pan inside and mix all the ingredients inside the pan. Cook on Baking mode at 200°C for thirty minutes. Divide the stew into bowls and serve.

(PREP + COOKING TIME: 40 MINUTES | SERVES: 4)

27

BEEF AND ADOBO SAUCE

Ingredients

- 450g beef stew meat, cubed
- 120g tomato sauce
- 2 garlic cloves, minced
- 30ml extra virgin olive oil
- 5g ginger, grated
- 10g adobo sauce
- Salt and black pepper for the taste

Preperation

1- Set the Foodi on Sauté mode, add the oil, heat, add the ginger, garlic combined with the meat and sauté for 5 minutes.

2- Add other ingredients, position the stress lid on and cook on High for 20 minutes. Release the load naturally for ten mins, divide into bowls and serve.

(PREP + COOKING TIME: 35 MINUTES | SERVES: 4)

28

GOAT CHOPS AND POTATOES

Ingredients

- 4 goat chops

- 450g gold potatoes, halved

- 1 yellow onion, chopped.

- 4g rosemary, chopped.

- 15ml extra virgin olive oil

- Salt and black pepper on the taste

Preperation

1- Put the reversible rack inside Foodi, add the baking pan inside and mix all of the ingredients inside the pan. Cook on Baking mode at 187°C for 25 minutes. Divide the amalgamation between plates and serve.

(PREP + COOKING TIME: 35 MINUTES | SERVES: 4)

29

BEEF CHOPS AND BASIL PESTO

Ingredients

- 4 beef chops
- 15ml organic olive oil
- 45g basil pesto
- Salt and black pepper for your taste

Preperation

1- In a bowl, mix every one of the ingredients and toss. Put the chops as part of your basket and cook on Air Fry at 195°C for 25 minutes.

2- Divide between plates and serve with a side salad.

(PREP + COOKING TIME: 35 MINUTES | SERVES: 4)

30

SIDE DISH RECIPES

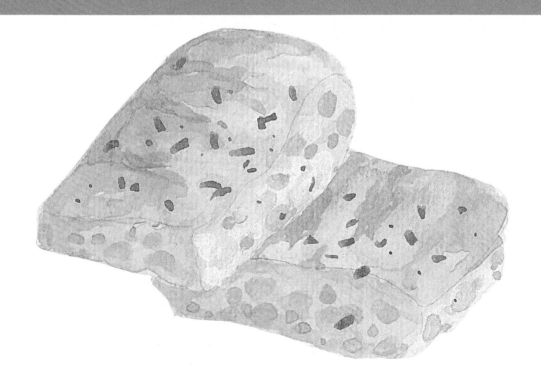

31

COCONUT POTATOES

Ingredients

- 450g gold potatoes; cut into wedges
- 250g coconut cream
- 15ml canola oil
- Salt and black pepper for the taste

Preperation

1. **Put the reversible rack inside the Foodi, add the baking pan inside and mix every one of the ingredients inside the pan.**

2. **Set the gear on Baking mode and cook at 195°C for twenty minutes. Divide between plates and serve as a side dish.**

(PREP + COOKING TIME: 25 MINUTES | SERVES: 4)

32

HERBED SQUASH

Ingredients

- 900g squash; peeled and cubed
- A drizzle of extra virgin olive oil
- 6g mixed herbs; dried
- 3g parsley; chopped.
- Salt and black pepper for that taste

Preperation

1. *In your Machine's basket combine all of the ingredients, toss and cook on Air Fry at 200°C for 20 minutes. Divide the squash between plates and serve as a side dish.*

(PREP + COOKING TIME: HALF AN HOUR | SERVES: 4)

33

GREEN BEANS

Ingredients

- 450g green beans.
- 3 garlic cloves; minced
- 15ml extra virgin olive oil
- Juice of merely one lime

Preperation

1. *In your Machine's basket, combine each of the ingredients, toss and cook on Air Fry at 187°C for fifteen minutes. Divide between plates and serve as a side dish.*

(PREP + COOKING TIME: 25 MINUTES | SERVES: 4)

34

GARLIC KALE SAUTÉ

Ingredients

- 200g kale leaves; torn
- 30g garlic; minced
- 30ml essential olive oil
- Salt and black pepper for the taste

Preperation

1. *In your Foodi, combine all of the ingredients, toss, position pressure to succeed lid on and cook on High for 12 minutes. Release pressure naturally for ten mins, divide this mixture between plates and serve as a side dish.*

(PREP + COOKING TIME: 22 MINUTES | SERVES: 4)

35

ITALIAN POTATOES

Ingredients

- 450g gold potatoes; cut into chunks
- 45ml essential olive oil
- 30g cheddar; grated
- 5g Italian seasoning
- A pinch of salt and black pepper

Preperation

1. In a bowl, mix the potatoes with the ingredients except the cheese, toss and put them with your Foodi's basket.

2. Set the device on Air Fry, cook the potatoes at 200°C for twenty or so minutes, divide between plates and serve with cheddar sprinkled ahead.

(PREP + COOKING TIME: HALF AN HOUR | SERVES: 4)

VEGETABLE RECIPES

37

ARTICHOKES AND BROCCOLI

Ingredients

- 340g artichoke hearts; trimmed
- 4 garlic cloves; chopped.
- 1 broccoli head; florets separated
- 30ml essential olive oil
- 6g chives; chopped.
- Salt and black pepper towards taste

Preperation

1- Put the reversible rack inside Foodi, add the baking pan and mix all the ingredients inside. Cook on Baking mode at 195°C for quarter-hour, divide between plates and serve.

(PREP + COOKING TIME: 20 MINUTES | SERVES: 4)

38

CELERIAC AND LEMON SAUCE

Ingredients

- 1 celeriac; cut into wedges
- Lemon zest of 2 lemons; grated
- Juice of 1/2 lemon
- 2g rosemary; chopped.
- 30ml extra virgin olive oil
- Salt and black pepper towards the taste

Preperation

1- In your Foodi, combine all the ingredients, place the pressure lid on and cook on High for quarter-hour. Release the strain fast for 5 minutes, divide everything between plates and serve.

(PREP + COOKING TIME: TWENTY MINUTES | SERVES: 4)

39

BEET AND FENNEL

Ingredients

- 450g beets; peeled and cut into wedges
- 2 navel oranges; peeled and cut into segments
- 400ml coconut milk
- 1 fennel bulb; thinly sliced
- 30ml orange juice
- 4g orange zest; grated
- 30ml extra virgin organic olive oil
- Salt and black pepper on the taste

Preperation

1- Put the reversible rack inside Foodi, add the baking pan and mix every one of the ingredients inside. Cook on Baking mode at 200°C for 25 minutes, divide between plates and serve.

(PREP + COOKING TIME: 25 MINUTES | SERVES: 4)

40

ASPARAGUS AND PESTO

Ingredients

- 450g asparagus; trimmed
- 60ml freshly squeezed fresh lemon juice
- 250g heavy cream
- 30g basil; chopped.
- 30g parsley; chopped.
- 12g chives; chopped.
- 2 garlic cloves minced
- A drizzle of organic essential olive oil

Preperation

1- In a blender, mix the parsley with each of the ingredients except the asparagus and pulse well.

2- Put the reversible rack inside Foodi, add the baking pan and mix the asparagus using the pesto inside. Cook on Baking mode at 200°C for a quarter-hour, divide everything between plates and serve.

(PREP + COOKING TIME: TWENTY OR SO MINUTES | SERVES: 4)

41

BUTTERY CABBAGE

Ingredients

- 1 green cabbage head shredded.
- 60g butter; melted
- 15g smoked paprika
- Salt and black pepper for the taste

Preperation

1- In your Foodi, mix every one of the ingredients, position pressure to succeed lid on and cook on High for 12 minutes. Release pressure fast for 5 minutes, divide everything between plates and serve.

(PREP + COOKING TIME: 17 MINUTES | SERVES: 4)

42

SNACK & APPETIZER RECIPES

43

BALSAMIC PARSNIPS CHIPS

Ingredients

- 4 parsnips; thinly sliced
- 30ml balsamic vinegar
- 30mlessential olive oil
- Salt and black pepper on the taste

Preperation

1. Put the Foodi's basket inside and mix each of the ingredients within it. Cook the chips on Air Fry at 195°C for twenty or so minutes. Divide into cups and serve as a snack.

(PREP + COOKING TIME: A HALF-HOUR | SERVES: 4)

44

MINTY TURKEY BITES

Ingredients

- 1 big turkey breast; skinless, boneless, and cubed
- 80ml Chicken broth
- 2g mint; chopped.
- 30ml essential extra virgin olive oil

Preperation

1. In your Ninja Foodi Max Smartlid, combine every one of the ingredients, toss, set your machine on Baking mode and cook at 200°C for 20 minutes. Divide into bowls and serve as a snack.

(PREP + COOKING TIME: A HALF-HOUR | SERVES: 4)

45

LAMB BITES

Ingredients

- 140g lamb stew meat; cubed

- 1 yellow onion; chopped.

- 50ml pomegranate juice

- 15ml extra virgin olive oil

- 3g garlic; minced

- Salt and black pepper towards the taste

Preperation

1. Set the Foodi on Sauté mode, add the oil, heat, add the garlic, onion, salt and pepper and sauté for 3 minutes.

2. Add the meat cubes along with the pomegranate juice, toss, position pressure to succeed lid on, and cook on High for 15 minutes. Release the strain fast for 6 minutes, divide the bites into bowls and serve.

(PREP + COOKING TIME: 26 MINUTES | SERVES: 9)

46

BUTTERY CHICKEN BITES

Ingredients

- 450g chicken white meat; skinless, boneless, and cubed
- 10g butter; melted
- 10g garlic powder
- Salt and black pepper for the taste

Preperation

1. In a bowl, mix all of the ingredients and transfer them to your Foodi's basket. Cook the chicken bites on Air Fry at 195°C for a quarter-hour. Divide into bowls and serve as a snack.

(PREP + COOKING TIME: 20 MINUTES | SERVES: 4)

47

COCONUT CARROT CHIPS

Ingredients

- 450g carrots; thinly sliced
- 170g coconut; shredded
- 2 eggs; whisked
- Salt and black pepper towards taste

Preperation

1. Put the coconut in a bowl and also the eggs blended with salt and pepper inside a different one.

2. Dredge the carrot chips in eggs then in coconut and hang them with your Foodi's basket. Cook the chips on Air Fry at 195°C for 20 mins and serve as a snack.

(PREP + COOKING TIME: 25 MINUTES | SERVES: 4)

48

DESSERT RECIPES

49

CHERRY CAKE

Ingredients

- 280g cherries; pitted and sliced
- 180g buttermilk
- 120g butter; soft
- 80g sugar
- 125g white flour
- 2 eggs; whisked
- Cooking spray

Preperation

1- In a bowl, mix every one of the ingredients except the cooking spray and stir rather well.

2- Put the reversible rack inside Foodi, add the wedding cake pan inside and grease it with cooking spray.

3- Pour the cake mix inside and cook it on Baking mode at 180°C for a half-hour. Cool the dessert down, slice, and serve.

(PREP + COOKING TIME: 35 MINUTES | SERVES: 6)

50

CRANBERRIES CREAM

Ingredients

- 450g cream cheese; soft
- 200g cranberry sauce
- 120g sugar

Preperation

1- In a bowl, combine all the ingredients, whisk well and pour into 4 ramekins. Put the reversible rack inside Foodi, squeeze ramekins inside, set your machine on Baking mode and cook at 150°C for a quarter-hour. Serve the cream cold.

(PREP + COOKING TIME: TWENTY MINUTES | SERVES: 4)

51

PLUMS AND CREAM CHEESE

Ingredients

- 450g plums; stones removed and halved
- 120g cream cheese; soft
- 6 eggs; whisked
- 75g sugar

Preperation

1- In a ramekin, combine all the ingredients and stir well.

2- Put the reversible rack within the Foodi machine, add the ramekin inside, set the pot on Baking mode, and cook at 165°C for a quarter-hour. Divide the amalgamation into cups and serve.

(PREP + COOKING TIME: 20 MINUTES | SERVES: 4)

52

PEAR PIE

Ingredients

- 4 pears; peeled, cored, and cubed
- 20cm pie crust dough
- 120g white sugar
- 45g sugar
- 15g butter; soft
- 15ml lemon juice
- 2g lemon zest; grated
- 5ml vanilla flavoring
- Cooking spray

Preperation

1- Grease your Foodi's cake pan with all the cooking spray and arrange the pie crust dough inside. In a bowl, mix the rest of the ingredients, whisk and pour to the pan.

2- Put the reversible rack inside Foodi, add the baking pan inside and cook on Baking mode at 180°C for 40 minutes. Cool the pie down, slice and serve.

(PREP + COOKING TIME: 45 MINUTES | SERVES: 4)

53

VANILLA PUDDING

Ingredients

- 120g white sugar
- 500ml milk
- 20g cornstarch
- 15g butter; melted
- 5ml vanilla flavoring

Preperation

1- In a bowl, mix all the ingredients, whisk well and pour this mixture into 4 ramekins.

2- Put the reversible rack inside Foodi, position the ramekins inside, set your machine on Baking mode, cook the puddings at 175°C for 25 minutes and serve cold.

(PREP + COOKING TIME: AROUND 30 MINUTES | SERVES: 4)

My Own Space!

54

Recipe Name:

Ingredients

Preperation

READY IN ABOUT:

SERVINGS:

55

Recipe Name:

Ingredients

➡️
➡️
➡️
➡️
➡️
➡️
➡️
➡️
➡️
➡️
➡️
➡️
➡️
➡️
➡️
➡️

READY IN ABOUT:

SERVINGS:

Preperation

56

Recipe Name:

Ingredients

➡
➡
➡
➡
➡
➡
➡
➡
➡
➡
➡
➡
➡
➡
➡
➡

READY IN ABOUT:

SERVINGS:

Preperation

57

Recipe Name:

Ingredients

➡
➡
➡
➡
➡
➡
➡
➡
➡
➡
➡
➡
➡
➡
➡
➡
➡

Preperation

READY IN ABOUT:

SERVINGS:

58

Recipe Name:

Ingredients

Preperation

READY IN ABOUT:

SERVINGS:

59

Recipe Name:

Ingredients

Preperation

READY IN ABOUT:

SERVINGS:

60

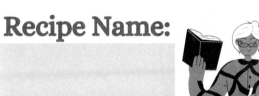

Recipe Name:

Ingredients

➡️
➡️
➡️
➡️
➡️
➡️
➡️
➡️
➡️
➡️
➡️
➡️
➡️
➡️
➡️
➡️
➡️

READY IN ABOUT:

SERVINGS:

Preperation

61

Recipe Name:

Ingredients

➡️
➡️
➡️
➡️
➡️
➡️
➡️
➡️
➡️
➡️
➡️
➡️
➡️
➡️
➡️
➡️
➡️

READY IN ABOUT:

SERVINGS:

Preperation

62

Recipe Name:

Ingredients

➡️
➡️
➡️
➡️
➡️
➡️
➡️
➡️
➡️
➡️
➡️
➡️
➡️
➡️
➡️
➡️
➡️

READY IN ABOUT:

SERVINGS:

Preperation

63

Recipe Name:

Ingredients

⇒
⇒
⇒
⇒
⇒
⇒
⇒
⇒
⇒
⇒
⇒
⇒
⇒
⇒
⇒
⇒
⇒

READY IN ABOUT:

SERVINGS:

Preperation

Printed in Great Britain
by Amazon

79298460R00045